Cross Stitch

Bright Blooms

2

9

Brighten up with these cheerful designs!

12

14

LEISURE ARTS, INC. • Maumelle, Arkansas

my journal

Flowery Ensemble

Designed by Joan Elliott

Add some whimsy to your life with this bright tote and coordinating mobile phone case, key ring, and journal!

Tote Stitch Count = 119w × 159h
Mobile Phone Case
Stitch Count = 25w × 41h
Key Ring Stitch Count = 29w × 28h
Journal Stitch Count = 43w × 69h

FABRIC SIZE

- One 11½" × 14½" (29.2cm × 36.8cm) 14-ct. Grasshopper Bright Ideas Aida Shoulder Bag by Charles Craft
- One 8" × 8" (20.3cm × 20.3cm) piece of 14-ct. Grasshopper Bright Ideas Aida by Charles Craft for mobile phone case
- One 8" × 8" (20.3cm × 20.3cm) piece of 14-ct. Grasshopper Bright Ideas Aida by Charles Craft for key ring
- One 10" × 12" (25.4cm × 30.5cm) piece of 14-ct. Grasshopper Bright Ideas Aida by Charles Craft for journal

DESIGN SIZE

- Tote = 8½" × 11⅜" (21.6cm × 28.9cm)
- Mobile Phone Case = 1¾" × 2⅞" (4.4cm × 7.3cm)
- Key Ring = 2⅛" × 2" (5.4cm × 5.1cm)
- Journal = 3⅛" × 5" (7.9cm × 12.7cm)

MOBILE PHONE CASE FINISHING MATERIALS

- One 9" x 12" (22.9cm × 30.5cm) piece of bright pink felt
- Lightweight iron-on interfacing
- Fusible web
- Matching sewing thread
- Pinking shears
- One small decorative button

KEY RING FINISHING MATERIALS

- One acrylic key ring with 2½"-diameter design area
- Lightweight iron-on interfacing
- Colored paper

JOURNAL FINISHING MATERIALS

- One 5½" × 8½" (14cm × 21.6cm) journal
- 20" (51cm) length of bright pink rickrack
- ½ yard of ¼"-wide grosgrain ribbon
- One small decorative button
- Lightweight iron-on interfacing
- Permanent fabric glue

GENERAL INSTRUCTIONS

Center the design and begin stitching. Use three strands of cotton or metallic embroidery floss to work cross stitches, three-quarter cross stitches, half cross stitches, and quarter cross stitches. Work backstitches with one strand of cotton or metallic embroidery floss. Use one strand of cotton embroidery floss to work French knots. Carefully press the needlework from the back, using a pressing cloth to protect the metallic floss.

MOBILE PHONE CASE FINISHING INSTRUCTIONS

Note: Carefully measure your mobile phone before starting this project, making any size adjustments as necessary. The measurements given are suitable for a phone up to 2¼" × 4½". Trim the needlework to five rows from the design area on all sides. Using matching sewing thread, machine-stitch a line one row from the design on all sides. To create a fringe, gently pull out three rows of fabric threads from all four sides.

Cut a piece of felt 4" × 12". Fold over by 5" lengthwise, leaving a 2" flap at the top. Stitch the long sides from the bottom of the flap with a ½" seam allowance. Turn the felt right side out and clip the flap ½" from the finished sides. Pink the top edge of the flap and fold to the back.

Cut a piece of iron-on interfacing to the size of the design area and fuse it to the wrong side of the needlework. Use a pressing cloth to protect the metallic floss. Using the sewing lines created for the fringe as a guide, cut a piece of fusible web to match.

Place the web between the needlework and the finished case and fuse using a pressing cloth. Attach a button to the top center of the back of the case where the flap meets the back and cut a slit in the flap to accommodate the button.

KEY RING FINISHING INSTRUCTIONS

Cut a piece of iron-on interfacing 1" larger than the diameter of the needlework. Center the interfacing on the wrong side of the needlework and fuse to the needlework fabric using a pressing cloth. Center the removable back of the key ring over the needlework and trace the circle outline onto the needlework fabric. Carefully cut along the line. Cut a piece of colored paper the same size as the needlework circle. Place the needlework inside the key ring with the colored paper behind it to conceal the back of the stitching. Snap the acrylic backing in place.

(continued on page 6)

Tote

CROSS STITCH

ANCHOR		DMC	COLOR
002	•	White	White
403	X	310	Black
062	G	603	Cranberry
050	H	605	Very Light Cranberry
308	V	782	Dark Topaz
256	K	906	Medium Parrot Green
881	S	945	Tawny
1010	P	951	Light Tawny
316	B	971	Pumpkin
298	A	972	Dark Canary
306	T	3820	Dark Straw
100	E	3837	Ultra Dark Lavender
1089	D	3843	Electric Blue

DMC LIGHT EFFECTS FLUORESCENTS		COLOR
E1010	Z	Tropical Pink
E1020	N	Bright Orange
E1040	J	Electric Blue
E1050	C	Luminous Lavender

FRENCH KNOT

ANCHOR		DMC	COLOR
403	•	310	Black

BACKSTITCH

ANCHOR		DMC	COLOR
403	—	310	Black

DMC LIGHT EFFECTS FLUORESCENTS		COLOR
E1010	—	Tropical Pink

Bright blue area indicates last row of previous section of design.

(continued from page 3)

JOURNAL FINISHING INSTRUCTIONS

Cut a piece of iron-on interfacing 1" larger than the stitched design on all sides. Center the interfacing on the wrong side of the needlework and fuse to the needlework fabric, using a pressing cloth to protect the metallic floss. Trim to five rows beyond the design on all sides. Center the prepared cross-stitch on the journal cover and attach using permanent fabric glue. Starting at the center bottom, attach rickrack with a thin line of glue, turning the corners as you go and covering the edge of the needlework fabric. Glue a small button where the rickrack ends meet. Open the front cover and run a line of glue along the inner edge, attaching the length of ribbon to create a handy bookmark.

CROSS STITCH

ANCHOR		DMC	COLOR
002	•	White	White
403	X	310	Black
062	G	603	Cranberry
050	H	605	Very Light Cranberry
308	V	782	Dark Topaz
256	K	906	Medium Parrot Green
881	S	945	Tawny
1010	P	951	Light Tawny
316	B	971	Pumpkin
298	A	972	Dark Canary
306	T	3820	Dark Straw
100	E	3837	Ultra Dark Lavender
1089	D	3843	Electric Blue

DMC LIGHT EFFECTS FLUORESCENTS		COLOR
E1010	Z	Tropical Pink
E1020	N	Bright Orange
E1040	J	Electric Blue
E1050	C	Luminous Lavender

FRENCH KNOT

ANCHOR		DMC	COLOR
403	•	310	Black

BACKSTITCH

ANCHOR		DMC	COLOR
403	—	310	Black

DMC LIGHT EFFECTS FLUORESCENTS		COLOR
E1010	—	Tropical Pink

Bright blue area indicates last row of previous section of design.

Project Tip

Stitching on Pre-Finished Items
For easier stitching, it is best to not wash pre-finished items before stitching, unless otherwise recommended by the manufacturer. The sizing in the fabric allows the piece to hold its shape during stitching. When finished, wash if desired, always following the manufacturer's instructions for fabric care.

Mobile Phone Case

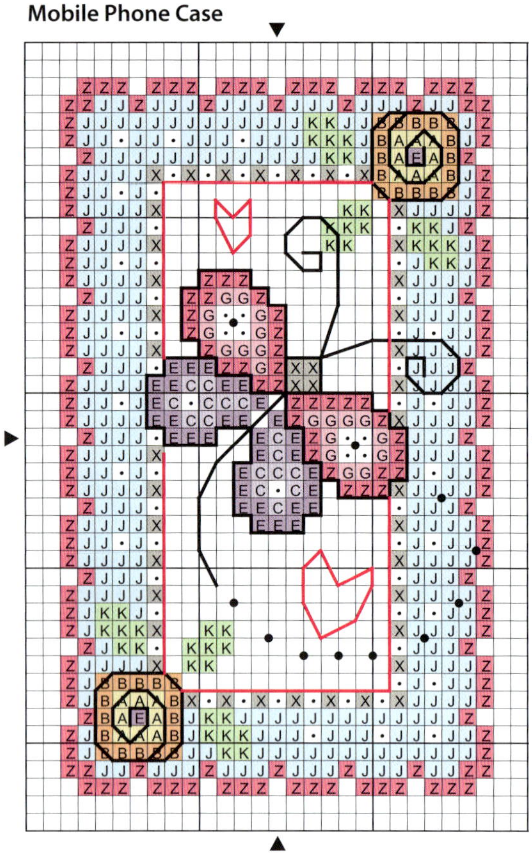

Journal

Key Ring

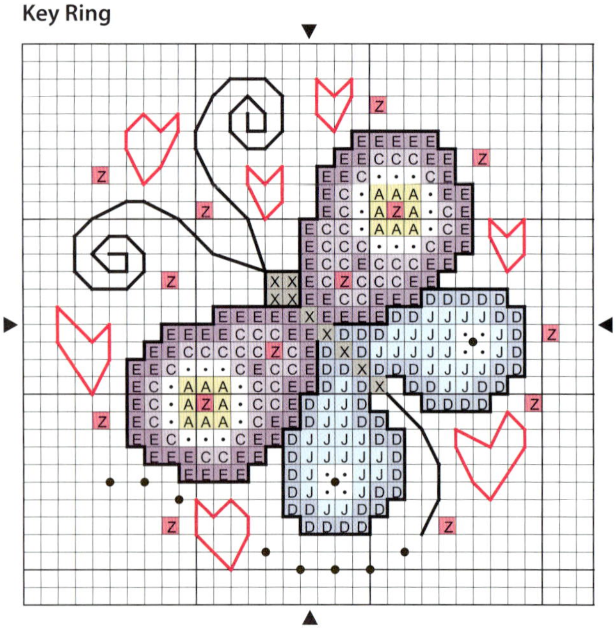

CROSS STITCH

ANCHOR		DMC	COLOR
002	•	White	White
403	X	310	Black
062	G	603	Cranberry
050	H	605	Very Light Cranberry
256	K	906	Medium Parrot Green
316	B	971	Pumpkin
298	A	972	Dark Canary
100	E	3837	Ultra Dark Lavender
1089	D	3843	Electric Blue

DMC LIGHT EFFECTS FLUORESCENTS		COLOR
E1010	Z	Tropical Pink
E1020	N	Bright Orange
E1040	J	Electric Blue
E1050	C	Luminous Lavender

FRENCH KNOT

ANCHOR		DMC	COLOR
403	•	310	Black
100	•	3837	Ultra Dark Lavender

BACKSTITCH

ANCHOR		DMC	COLOR
403	—	310	Black
100	—	3837	Ultra Dark Lavender

DMC LIGHT EFFECTS FLUORESCENTS		COLOR
E1010	—	Tropical Pink

Spring Fling

Designed by Sharon Pope

This exuberant piece, loaded with color and cheerful patterns, will make a lively addition to your home!

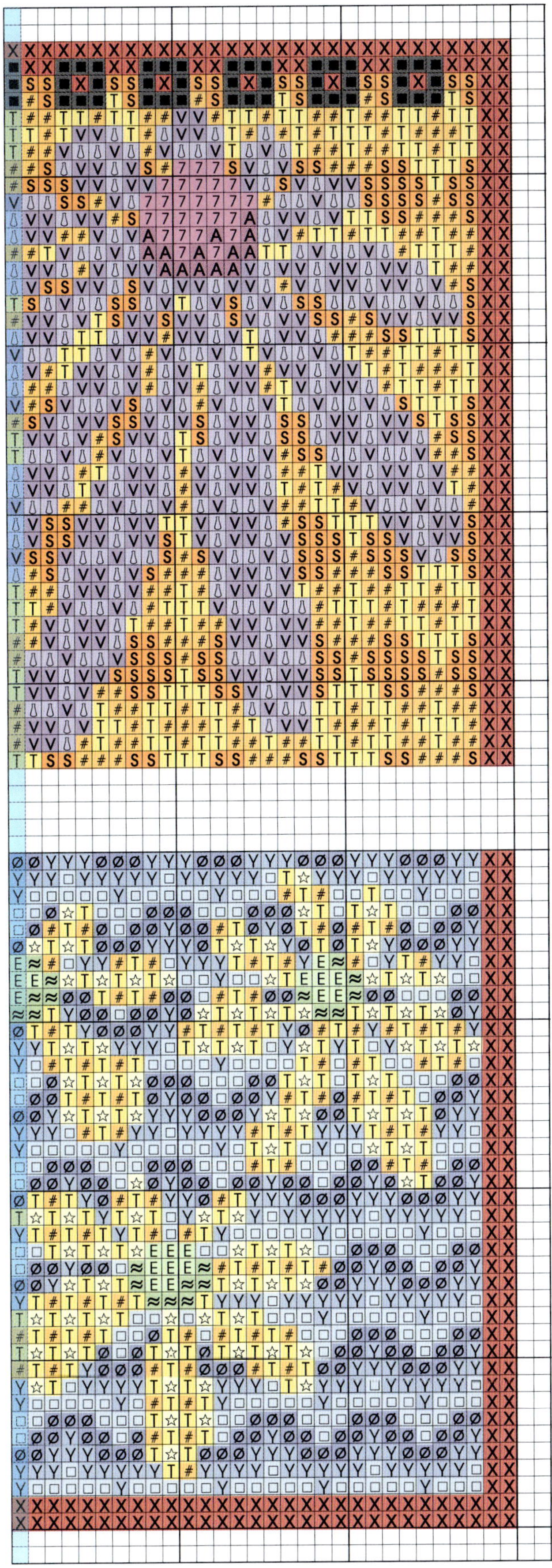

Stitch Count = 98w × 88h

FABRIC SIZE

- One 13" × 13" (33.0cm × 33.0cm) piece of 14-ct. white aida

DESIGN SIZE

- 7" × 6¼" (17.8cm × 15.9cm)

Note: The frame is no longer available through retailers. To mimic the black lines, stitch between the floral designs in black, or cut a black mat to match the areas between the floral designs and then frame.

CROSS STITCH

ANCHOR		DMC	COLOR
403	■	310	Black
9046	X	321	Christmas Red
119	V	333	Very Dark Blue Violet
118	[illegible]	340	Medium Blue Violet
290	T	444	Dark Lemon
288	☆	445	Light Lemon
062	[illegible]	603	Cranberry
055	U	604	Light Cranberry
088	7	718	Plum
161	□	813	Light Blue
164	Ø	824	Very Dark Blue
162	Y	826	Medium Blue
257	B	905	Dark Parrot Green
256	≈	906	Medium Parrot Green
255	E	907	Light Parrot Green
1029	A	915	Dark Plum
316	S	971	Pumpkin
298	#	972	Dark Canary
087	⊙	3607	Light Plum

Bright blue area indicates last row of previous section of design.

Bright Bookmarks

Designed by Joan Elliott

Keeping your place in a favorite book is easy with these vibrant designs! Share the joy of reading when you give someone a cute cross stitched bookmark.

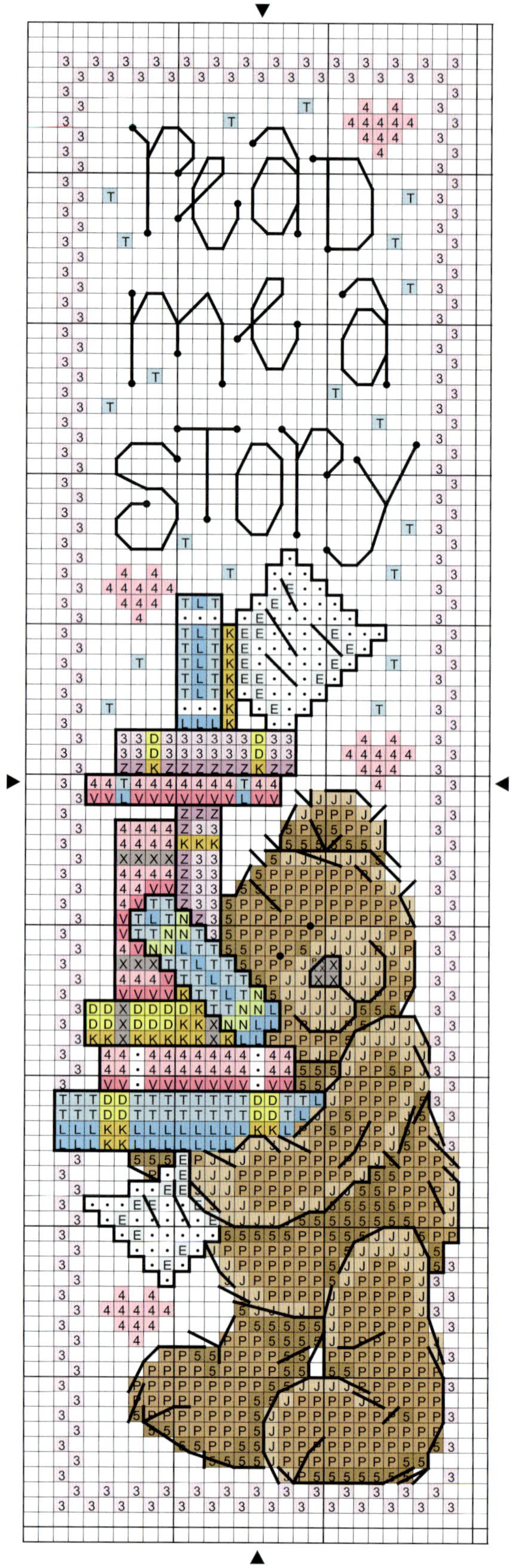

Teddy Bear Bookmark
Stitch Count = 27w × 97h
Sunflower Bookmark
Stitch Count = 27w × 98h
So Many Books Bookmark
Stitch Count = 27w × 98h

FABRIC SIZE

- 2½" × 8" (6.4cm × 20.3cm) pre-finished 14-ct. Grasshopper, Polar Ice, and Lemon Twist Bright Ideas Aida Bookmarks by Charles Craft

DESIGN SIZE (each design)

Approximately 2" × 7" (5.1cm × 17.8cm)

INSTRUCTIONS

Center the Teddy Bear design on the Grasshopper bookmark, the Sunflower design on the Polar Ice bookmark, and the So Many Books design on the Lemon Twist bookmark and begin stitching. Work cross stitches, three-quarter cross stitches, half cross stitches, and quarter cross stitches with two strands of cotton embroidery floss. Use one strand of cotton embroidery floss to work backstitches and French knots. Lightly press the needlework from the back.

CROSS STITCH

ANCHOR		DMC	COLOR
002	•	White	White
289	7	307	Lemon
403	X	310	Black
399	U	318	Light Steel Gray
398	E	415	Pearl Gray
310	S	434	Light Brown
098	3	553	Violet
059	V	600	Very Dark Cranberry
063	4	602	Medium Cranberry
062	6	603	Cranberry
891	J	676	Light Old Gold
901	5	680	Dark Old Gold
890	P	729	Medium Old Gold
359	I	801	Dark Coffee Brown
256	Y	906	Medium Parrot Green
255	N	907	Light Parrot Green
881	G	945	Tawny
1010	A	951	Light Tawny
298	K	972	Dark Canary
297	D	973	Bright Canary
100	Z	3837	Ultra Dark Lavender
410	L	3844	Dark Bright Turquoise
1090	T	3846	Light Bright Turquoise

FRENCH KNOT

ANCHOR		DMC	COLOR
403	•	310	Black

BACKSTITCH

ANCHOR		DMC	COLOR
403	—	310	Black

Mini Flower Trio

Designed by Angie Williams and Lynda Watkins

Three contemporary floral designs stitched on bright green and orange fabric will bring a burst of color to any room. Finished as a triptych, this piece creates big impact from the trio of easy-to-stitch designs.

Stitch Count (each design) = 22w × 37h

FABRIC SIZE

- Two 9" × 11" (22.9cm × 27.9cm) pieces of 14-ct. Tropical Green Aida by Wichelt Imports
- One 9" × 11" (22.9cm x 27.9cm) piece of 14-ct. Tropical Orange Aida by Wichelt Imports

DESIGN SIZE (each design)

- 1½" x 2⅝" (3.8cm x 6.7cm)

Project Tip

Prevent Twisting
During the movement of stitching, the needle naturally twists, which can cause loops and knots in the thread. To prevent this, work several stitches, then make note of which way the thread unwinds when you hang it straight down from your work. Give your needle a partial turn in that direction with each stitch to keep the thread from twisting.

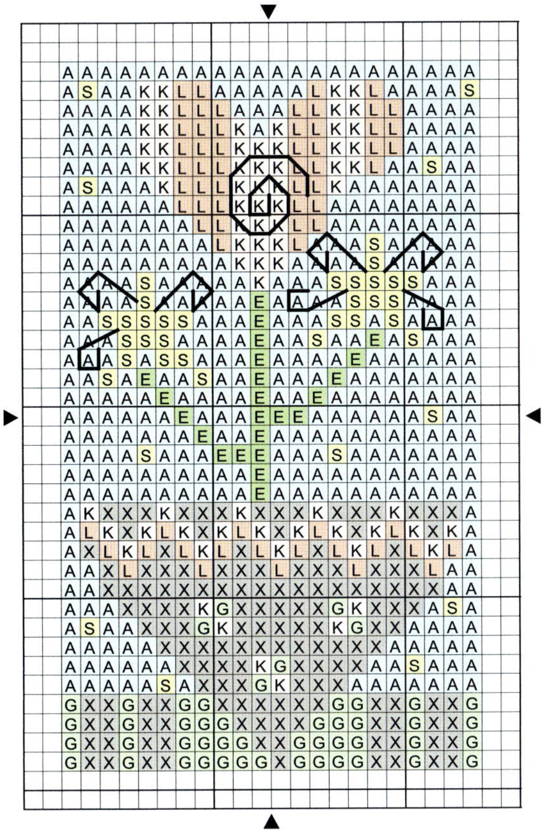

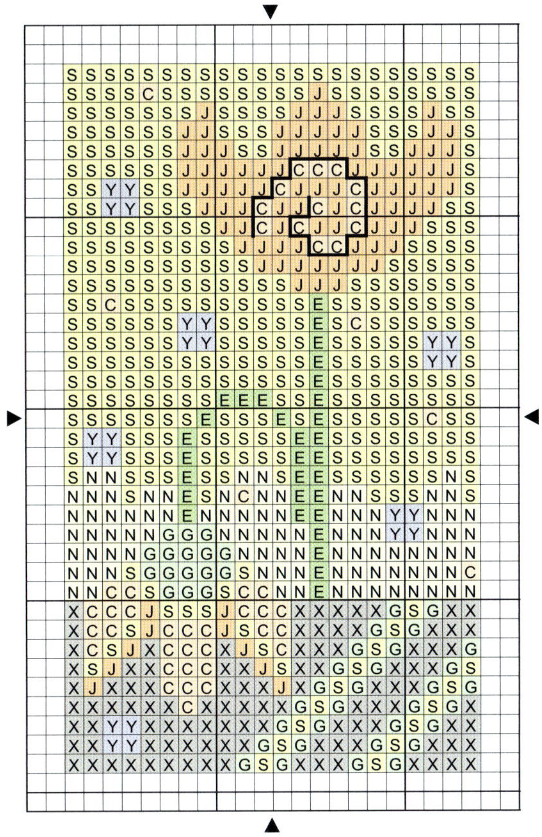

CROSS STITCH

ANCHOR		DMC	COLOR
403	X	310	Black
046	L	666	Bright Christmas Red
886	N	677	Very Light Old Gold
238	G	703	Chartreuse
323	C	722	Light Orange Spice
941	Y	792	Dark Cornflower Blue
258	E	904	Very Dark Parrot Green
1003	J	922	Light Copper
035	K	3705	Dark Melon
295	S	3822	Light Straw
1090	A	3846	Light Bright Turquoise

BACKSTITCH

ANCHOR		DMC	COLOR
403	———	310	Black

STRAIGHT STITCH

ANCHOR		DMC	COLOR
046	———	666	Bright Christmas Red

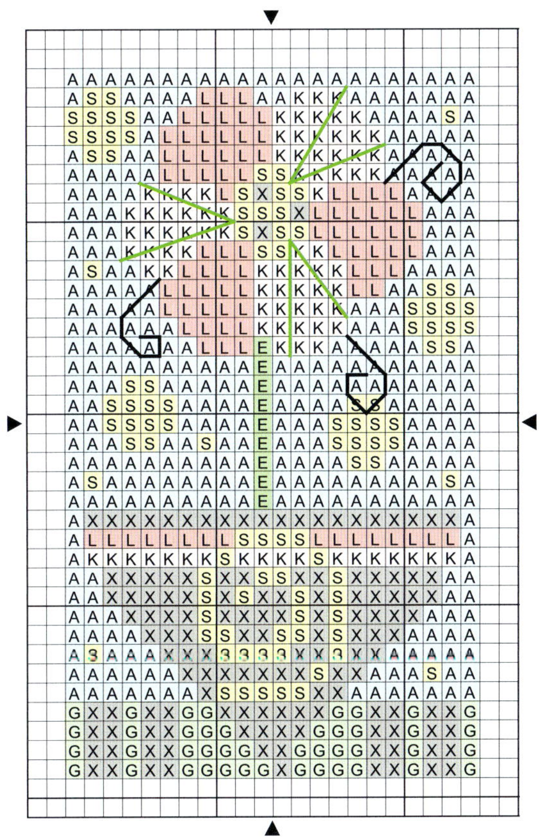

General Instructions

Getting Started

For most projects, the starting point is at the center. Every chart has arrows that indicate the horizontal and vertical centers. With your finger, trace along the grid to the point where the two centers meet. Compare a symbol at the center of the chart to the key and choose which floss color to stitch first. To find the center of the fabric, fold it into quarters and finger-crease.

Cut the floss into 15" lengths and separate all six strands. Recombine the appropriate number of strands and thread them into a blunt-tip needle. Unless otherwise indicated, use two strands of floss to work cross stitches, three-quarter cross stitches, half cross stitches, and quarter cross stitches, and use one strand of floss to work backstitches, straight stitches, and French knots.

To Secure Thread at the Beginning

The most common way to secure the beginning tail of the thread is to hold it on the wrong side of the fabric under the first four or five stitches.

To Secure Thread at the End

To finish, slip the threaded needle under previously stitched threads on the wrong side of the fabric for four or five stitches, weaving the thread back and forth a few times. Clip the thread.

Framing Your Pieces

Iron the finished needlework on the wrong side using a dry pressing cloth and medium temperature setting; do not steam. Accurately measure the length and width of your completed piece before purchasing a mat or frame. Consulting a professional framer or art supply store to mat and frame your design is recommended.

Cross Stitch

Make one cross stitch for each symbol on the chart. For horizontal rows, stitch the first diagonal of each stitch in the row. Work back across the row, completing each stitch. On most linen and evenweave fabrics, work the stitches over two threads as shown in the diagram. For aida cloth, each stitch fills one square. You also can work cross stitches in the reverse direction. Remember to embroider the stitches uniformly—that is, always work the top half of each stitch in the same direction.

Quarter and Three-Quarter Cross Stitches

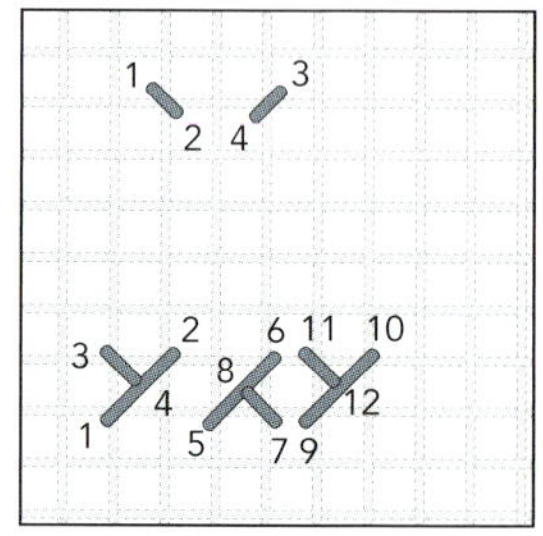

To obtain rounded shapes in a design, use quarter and three-quarter cross stitches. On linen and evenweave fabrics, a quarter stitch will extend from the corner to the center intersection of the threads. To make quarter cross stitches on aida cloth, estimate the center of the square. Three-quarter cross stitches combine a quarter cross stitch with a half cross stitch. Both stitches may slant in any direction.

Half Cross Stitches

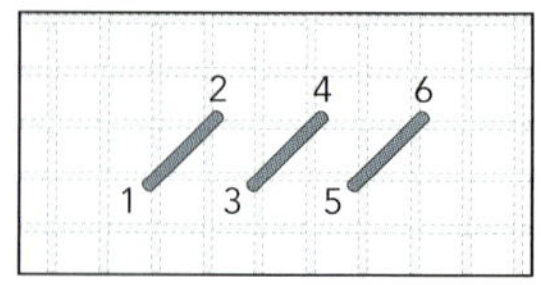

A half cross stitch is a single diagonal or half a cross stitch. They are indicated on the chart by a diagonal colored symbol.

Backstitches

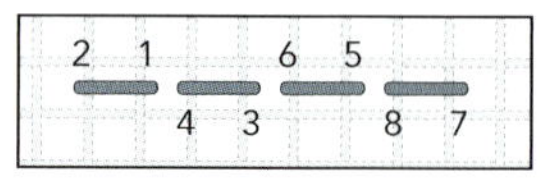

Working from right to left, bring the needle up from the back side of the fabric, one stitch length from your starting point. Begin the next stitch by inserting the needle at your starting point and back up two stitch lengths away. Continue, keeping all the stitches the same length.

French Knot

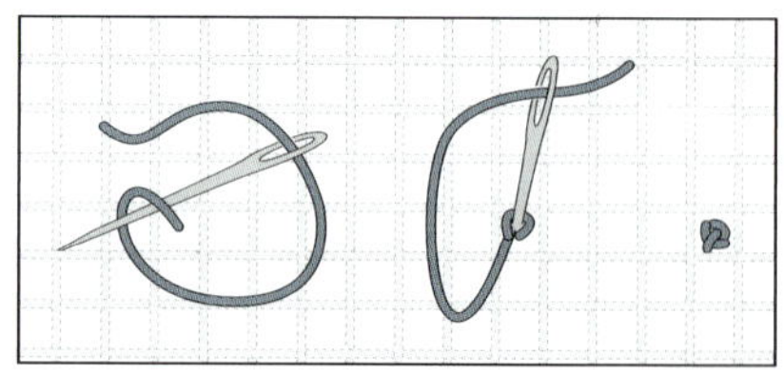

Bring the threaded needle through the fabric and wrap the floss around the needle as shown. Tighten the twists and return the needle through the fabric in the same place. The floss will slide through the wrapped thread to make the knot.

Straight Stitches

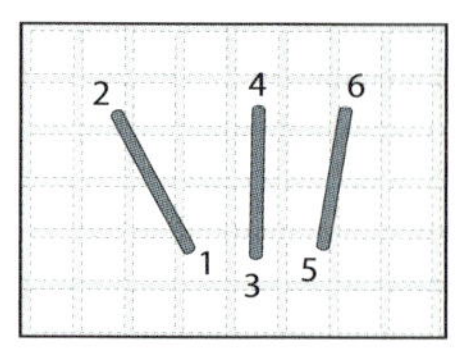

Bring the needle up from the back side of the fabric, then bring the needle down through the fabric in the desired spot to make a stitch of the desired length.

Produced by Herrschners, Inc., for distribution exclusively by Leisure Arts, Inc., 104 Champs Blvd., STE 100, Maumelle, AR 72113-6738, leisurearts.com.